THIS BOOK BELONGS TO:

_____

WELCOME TO FLORIDA

Dedicated to Katy and John.

All rights reserved.
No part of this book may be reproduced in any form or by any means, electronic or mechanical, and no photocopying or recording, unless you have written permission from the author.

ISBN 978-1-958985-24-3

Text copyright © 2024 by Mimi Jones

www.joeysavestheday.com

A Mimi Book

Juan Ponce de León, a Spanish explorer, is credited with the discovery of Florida. He named it La Florida, inspired by the lush, floral landscape and the Easter season. In Spanish, it is known as "Pascua Florida."

Florida was the twenty-seventh state to join the union. It officially joined on March 3, 1845.

Florida is located on the Southeastern coast of the United States and is bordered by two states: Alabama and Georgia.

Tallahassee, a city located in the state of Florida, officially became the capital in 1824.

Tallahassee, Florida, has an estimated population of around 201,730 people.

Florida, the 22nd largest state in the United States, is often described as being of medium size in comparison to other states.

Florida State Capital
400 S Monroe St
Tallahassee, FL 32399

There are about 21,538,180 people who live in Florida.

Fort Lauderdale, Florida

THE King OF

Wallace Amos Jr. was born in Tallahassee, Florida. He is renowned as the innovative mind behind the creation of the widely beloved Famous Amos chocolate chip cookies.

He was born July 1, 1936, to Wallace and Ruby Amos and lived in Tallahassee, Florida, until he was 12 years old.

Paul R. Sanberg, a well-known American scientist, was born in 1955 in Coral Gables, Florida. He has made important contributions to the field of science. His extensive scientific research has mainly focused on understanding how the human brain works, finding out why it deteriorates, and developing new treatments for different mental disorders.

FLORIDA

There are 67 counties in Florida.

Here is a list of 20 of those counties:

Alachua	Collier	Hamilton	Liberty
Baker	DeSoto	Hendry	Miami-Dade
Brevard	Escambia	Jackson	Palm Beach
Calhoun	Franklin	Lafayette	Suwannee
Citrus	Gilchrist	Lee	Walton

The John F. Kennedy Space Center, a renowned hub for space exploration and innovation, is strategically positioned in the picturesque coastal region of Cape Canaveral, Florida.

The historic St. Augustine Lighthouse, a towering beacon of maritime history, stands proudly in St. Augustine, Florida. It offers breathtaking views of the surrounding area and serves as a symbol of seafaring heritage.

EPCOT, short for Experimental Prototype Community of Tomorrow, is a unique and futuristic theme park nestled within the enchanting Walt Disney World Resort in Bay Lake, Florida.

Florida is home to an impressive collection of over 1200 golf courses, boasting the highest number of golf courses of any state in the country.

The official state bird of Florida is the northern mockingbird. This bird has a striking appearance, with feathers that range from grayish-brown to dark brown, adorned with patches of white. Its chest and underside are a soft, off-white color, adding to its distinctive and elegant look.

The official state flower of Florida is the Orange Blossom, which was designated as the state flower in 1909.

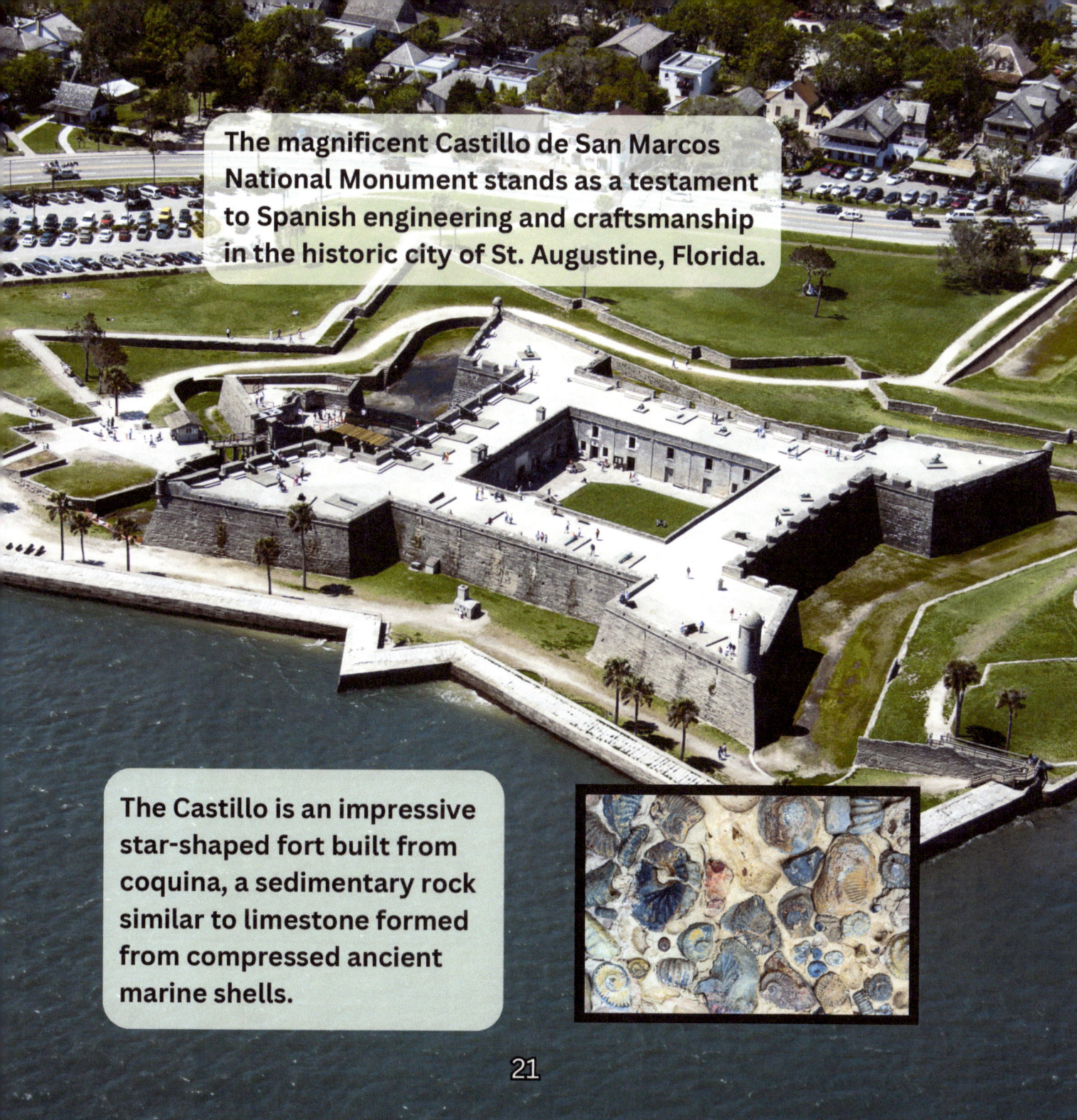

The magnificent Castillo de San Marcos National Monument stands as a testament to Spanish engineering and craftsmanship in the historic city of St. Augustine, Florida.

The Castillo is an impressive star-shaped fort built from coquina, a sedimentary rock similar to limestone formed from compressed ancient marine shells.

Some popular nicknames for Florida are the Sunshine State and the Alligator State.

State

State

The Florida state motto is In God We Trust.

The abbreviation for Florida is FL.

FL

The Florida state flag, which is currently in use, became the official flag on November 6, 1900. It has undergone several changes over the years.

Some animals that live in Florida are alligators, bears, dolphins, flamingos, panthers, pelicans, otters, and crocodiles.

Florida experiences extreme temperatures. The highest recorded was 109°F in Monticello, Florida, on June 29, 1931, and the lowest was -2°F in Tallahassee, Florida, on February 13, 1899.

Florida boasts an impressive coastline that stretches for 8,436 miles, making it the second-longest coastline in the United States.

Rainbow Springs State Park is a great place to visit. It is in Dunnellon, FL.

Some features of the park.

Hiking

Canoeing & Kayaking

Snorkeling

Swimming

Geocaching

Florida

The Palm Beaches in Florida are a beautiful tropical paradise. Their pristine beaches along the Atlantic coast offer a perfect mix of natural beauty and luxury.

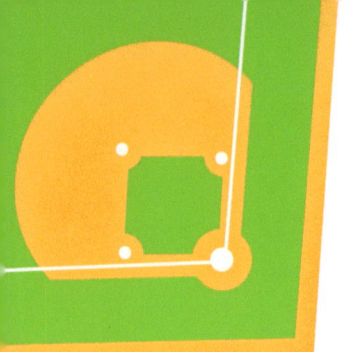   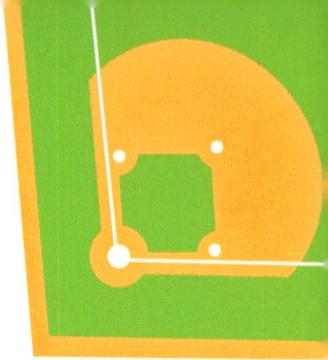

Florida boasts two MLB teams that light up the regular season: the Miami Marlins and the Tampa Bay Rays. The Marlins compete in the National League East division, while the Rays showcase their talents in the American League East division.

The Florida Gators, the University of Florida's football team, play their home games at Ben Hill Griffin Stadium, also known as "The Swamp," in Gainesville, Florida.

The University of Florida (UF) is a well-known public research university in Gainesville, Florida. It was founded in 1853 and is recognized for its excellent academics, advanced research, and active campus life.

Can you name these?

I hope you enjoyed
learning about
Florida.

To explore fun facts about the other 49 states, visit my website at www.joeysavestheday.com. You'll also find a wide variety of homeschool resources to support joyful learning at home. If you enjoyed this book, I would be grateful if you left a review. Your feedback truly helps. Thank you for your support!

Check out these other interesting books in the 50 States Fact Books Series!

www.mimibooks.com

www.ingramcontent.com/pod-product-compliance
Lightning Source LLC
Chambersburg PA
CBHW040027050426
42453CB00002B/33